Profiting From The Parables

by

Johnny Stringer

truth BOOKS

Guardian of Truth Foundation
CEI Bookstore
220 S. Marion St., Athens, AL 35611

ISBN 10: 1-58427-015-2

ISBN 13: 978-1-58427-0157

truth
BOOKS

Guardian of Truth Foundation
CEI Bookstore
220 S. Marion St., Athens, AL 35611
www.CEIbooks.com
1-855-49-BOOKS or 1-855-492-6657

Table of Contents

Dedication

To my parents, **Norbert and Jimmie Stringer**, this book is gratefully dedicated. To them I will always be indebted for their parental care and sacrifices and for their unconditional love.

The Sower
(Matt. 13:1-23; Mark 1:3-20; Luke 8:4-15)

Introduction

One of Jesus' teaching methods was to tell stories that illustrated spiritual truths. These true-to-life stories are called "parables." The word "parable" (*parabole*) denotes a comparison. Bruce says, "A parable is a saying or story that seeks to drive home a point the speaker wishes to emphasize by illustrating it from a familiar situation of common life" (*The Zondervan Pictorial Encyclopedia of the Bible*). This study does not discuss every saying that could be defined as a parable, but it includes most of the stories that people generally regard as parables.

The first parable the gospel records is about a sower who went forth to sow. Jesus spoke this parable, as well as others, from a ship that he used as a pulpit while he taught the multitude on the shore of the Sea of Galilee (Matt. 13:1-3; Mark 4:1-2; Luke 8:4).

After he had told the parable, his disciples asked him the reason for teaching in parables. Jesus' reply suggests that he did not intend for anyone other than genuine truth-seekers to understand his teachings. Those who were lacking in interest or hardened in heart would not get the point of the stories, but genuine truth-seekers would think, ask questions, and meditate on the stories so as to arrive at an understanding of the great principles that Jesus was illustrating (Matt. 13:10-17; Mark 4:10-13; Luke 8:18).

At the beginning of the study of the parables, one should remember that Jesus was seeking to illustrate certain points. We should not try to assign a meaning to every detail of the story. Rather, we should seek to determine the main points Jesus was illustrating.

The Parable and Its Interpretation

A man sows seed in various kinds of soil and the results depend on the nature of the soil. The Lord explains that the seed represents the word of God and the various kinds of soil represent various kinds of hearts. The effect of the word in one's life depends on the kind of heart he has.

This parable emphasizes the importance of the word in the conversion of sinners. The gospel is God's power unto salvation (Rom. 1:16; 1 Cor. 1:18). The word is that which touches men's hearts (Acts 2:37) and produces faith (Rom. 10:17; Acts 14:1). It works as seed within the heart to produce the change that is called the new birth (1 Pet. 1:23).

In the parable, the seed (representing the word) falls into four kinds of soil (representing four kinds of hearts):

1. The wayside. This is ground that is hard because it serves as a walkway. Because the seed cannot sink in, birds eat it and it produces no fruit. The wayside heart is the heart that does not allow the word to sink in. As the birds take the seed from the wayside soil, the devil takes the word from the unreceptive heart. This prevents the development of faith (Luke 8:12; Rom. 10:17). Prejudice, indifference, and an aversion to turning from evil are attitudes that can cause this condition.

2. Stony places. This denotes ground in which a shallow, underlying ledge of rock prevents the root from going deep. Though the seed comes up quickly, the new plant soon withers under the scorching sun. The one whose heart is represented by stony ground is one who quickly responds to the word, but his faith and commitment are shallow because the word is not deeply established in his heart. As the sun withers the plant that is not deeply rooted, tribulation and persecution destroy the convert in whom the word is not deeply established.

3. Thorny ground. The seed that falls among thorns is destroyed as the thorns choke it out. The thorns represent earthly concerns and the desire for wealth. These can fill one's heart and choke out the word's influence.

4. Good ground. The good ground represents the heart that hears and understands so that the word produces much good fruit in his life.

Questions

1. Where was Jesus when he delivered the Parable of the Sower? _____

   _____

2. What did the disciples ask Jesus?_____

   _____

3. Jesus said, "It is given unto you to know the mysteries of the _____

   _____ of _____, but to them it is not given."

   4. Those who closed their eyes to the truth were fulfilling the words of
   whose prophecy? _____

   5. What will be the result if people do not hear and understand (Mark
   4:12)? _____

   6. Every detail of a parable has a meaning, and we must discern that
   meaning if we are to understand the parable. True or False_____

   7. In the parable of the sower, the different kinds of soil represent different
   kinds of _____, and the _____ represents the word of God.

   8. What will determine the effect that the word of God has in your life?

   _____

   _____

   9. As the fowls devoured the seed that fell on the wayside ground, the
   _____ takes away the word when it does not sink into one's
   heart.

10. What are some attitudes that can prevent the word from sinking in?

    _____

    _____

11. According to Luke 8:12, a person will not develop faith if (a) God does
    not send the Spirit directly into his heart (b) the word is not allowed to
    sink into his heart. (Underline the correct answer.)

12. The seed that fell in stony ground quickly withered because it had no
    root and therefore lacked _____ (Luke 8:6).

13. The word must be deeply rooted in our hearts so that our commitment
    is strong and our faith unshakeable. Our commitment must be such

that we do not love _____ or _____ or _____ or
_____ more than Jesus, and we take up our _____
and follow him (Matt. 10:37-38).

14. If the word is deeply rooted in one's heart, he will not faint, for he will
realize that his afflictions are _____ in comparison to
the eternal _____ of _____ that awaits us (2 Cor.
4:16-18).

15. Are "thorns" that choke the word always things that, within themselves,
are sinful? _____

16. Luke describes the good ground as a heart that is _____
and _____.

Which Kind of Ground?

Read the description of each individual and tell which kind of ground represents that person's heart.

1. He spends so much time in the business he operates that he has no time
to study the Bible, assemble to worship, or teach his children about
God. _____

2. He has long been a member of a religious body that teaches false
doctrines, and he does not want to change. Hence, he will not listen to
those who attempt to show him what the Bible teaches. _____

3. He obeyed the gospel soon after hearing it; but when some began ridiculing him because he would not drink alcohol with them, he became
unfaithful to avoid the ridicule. _____

4. He listened to the gospel and accepted it even though it required him
to forsake the religion he had practiced for many years. His heart is
devoted to the service of God, and he stands for what is right regardless
of the opposition and ridicule he faces. _____

Two Parables Depicting the Final Separation of the Good From the Wicked

The Tares
(Matt. 13:24-30, 36-43)

Like many parables, this one begins with the words, "The kingdom of heaven is likened unto. . . ." This means that the kingdom, in some respect is comparable to the situation depicted in the story.

A man sows wheat in his field, but during the night, his enemy sows tares (weeds) in the midst of the wheat. The man's servants ask if he wants them to pull up the tares, but the man tells them to let the tares grow with the wheat; then in the time of harvest, the reapers will burn the tares and gather the wheat into the barn.

The wheat represents the children of the kingdom. The one who sows the wheat represents Christ, for Christ is the Savior whose work has resulted in men becoming citizens of the kingdom of heaven. The tares are the wicked. The enemy who sows the tares represents the devil, for the devil's efforts influence men unto wickedness. The field in which exist both wheat and tares, is the world; in the world both the godly and the wicked co-exist. The harvest is the end of the world and the reapers are the angels that Christ will use to separate eternally the wicked from the righteous.

The point of the parable is that Christ allows the wicked (tares) to exist in this world (the field) along with the citizens of the kingdom (wheat). This situation will continue until the end of the world (the harvest) when the angels (reapers) gather the wicked from among the citizens of the kingdom and cast them into a furnace of fire.

Some misuse the command to let the wheat and tares grow together. They argue that this command forbids one's exposing the errors of brethren and that it forbids congregational withdrawal from unrepentant brethren in sin. We are to let the tares grow undisturbed, according to this position.

In fact, this parable has nothing to do with the church's treatment of sinful brethren. Jesus is not discussing the righteous and wicked in the church. The field is the world (v. 38), not the church. Jesus is simply teaching that wicked people will exist in the world, along with citizens of the kingdom, until the end of the world. Then they will be removed from among the citizens of the kingdom and cast into the furnace of fire. One cannot change that. When ungodly brethren are rebuked or when a congregation withdraws from an unrepentant member, the separation forbidden in vv. 28-30 has not occurred. The wheat and tares are still growing together in the world (the field) and will continue to do so until God separates them at the end of the world.

The Net (Matt. 18:47-50)

The word here translated "net" denotes a seine or dragnet. This large net, having weights on the bottom and floats on the top, sweeps through the water catching all kinds of fish. The fishermen then draw the net to land, where they cull their catch. The good fish are put into vessels and taken to market, but the bad are thrown away.

The separating of the good fish from the bad illustrates the judgment that will occur at the end of the world. As the bad fish are taken from among the good, the wicked will be separated from the just and cast into the furnace of fire.

Questions

1. In the Parable of the Tares, who is represented by the wheat (good seed)? _____ The one who sowed the wheat? _____
2. When the enemy, who represents the _____, sowed tares in the midst of the wheat, what did the man's servants ask? _____

   _____
3. The man said to let the wheat and tares grow together until _____, which represents what? _____
4. The man said that he would tell the reapers (who represent _____) to gather the tares, bind them, and _____ them, but to gather the _____ into his barn.

5. In his explanation, Jesus said, "As therefore the tares are gathered and _____ in the _____; so shall it be in the end of this world."

6. Jesus will send forth his _____, and they will gather the wicked from among the citizens of his kingdom and cast them into a _____ of _____ (vv. 41-42).

7. The Bible does not contradict itself. In view of 2 Timothy 4:2, Ephesians 5:11, and Titus 1:10-13, is it possible that the Parable of the Tares is teaching us not to expose error or to rebuke those who teach and practice it? _____

_____

8. In view of 1 Corinthians 5:11 and 2 Thessalonians 3:6, 14-15, is it possible that the Parable of the Tares is forbidding a church to withdraw from unrepentant sinful members?_____

9. Jesus was teaching that he will allow the wicked to exist in the _____, along with the children of the _____, until the end of the world.

10. When we rebuke brethren in sin or when a church withdraws from ungodly members, the sinners (tares) (a) have been removed from the world (b) are still in the world along with the godly. Underline the correct answer._____

11. As the righteous live along with the wicked in this world, what function should the righteous be serving (Matt. 5:16; Phil. 2:15-16)? _____

_____

12. The Parable of the Tares depicts the devil as actively opposing Christ. Why should we be concerned (1 Pet. 5:8-9)? _____

_____

Are we capable of resisting him (Jas. 4:7)?_____

13. The Parable of the Net depicts fishermen catching all kinds of fish, then using all of them for the various purposes to which they were suited. True or False_____

14. The separating of the good fish from the bad illustrates the separation that will occur at the final judgment. True or False _____

15. The wicked will be cast into a _____ of _____.

16. When Jesus comes he will separate the righteous from the unrighteous as a shepherd separates _____ from _____ (Matt. 25:31-32).

17. To the wicked, Jesus will say, "Depart from me ye _____ into the _____ _____ prepared for the _____ and his _____" (Matt. 25:41)?

18. When the great separation occurs, some will go into punishment and others into life. What will be the duration of both the punishment and the life (Matt. 25:46)?_____

More Parables on the Kingdom

The Seed Growing (Mark 4:26-29)

The kingdom of Christ is not a political kingdom. It does not exist through military might but through the sowing of seed (the word of God) into the hearts of men (cf. the Parable of the Sower).

Jesus illustrates the manner in which the teaching of the word achieves its results. After a man sows seed, it eventually produces fruit, but the man does not understand how. The process is hidden from the eyes of men, but the results are apparent and the sower finally harvests the fruit. The visible results of the invisible process are gradual: First the blade (stem) appears, then the ear or head, and finally the seed that fills the ear. Similarly, when the word is sown into a man's heart, we do not see its working within the heart. But we see gradual results as the person's attitude changes, faith develops, he obeys the conditions to have his sins forgiven, and his character continues to become more godly as time goes by.

Through this process, Jesus establishes his rule in the hearts of men.

Two Parables on the Kingdom's Growth

The disciples could have become discouraged when people throughout the world were not suddenly and quickly brought into submission to the reign of Jesus. These parables should have helped them.

The Mustard Seed (Matt. 13:31-32; Mark 4:30-32). The mustard seed was generally the smallest of the seeds that men sowed in their gardens. It was used proverbially to refer to a thing that was tiny. From this tiniest of seeds, however, there came a plant that was larger than all the other garden plants — so large in fact that it could even be called a tree. Today, mustard in Palestine grows to a height of over ten feet, sometimes even reaching fifteen feet. Like the mustard seed, the kingdom of God would be small in its beginning, but it would grow as the gospel was proclaimed far and wide.

The Leaven (Matt. 13:33). The spreading of the kingdom would be like the spreading of leaven through a batch of dough. Whereas leaven is sometimes used to illustrate the spreading of evil (Matt. 16:6, 12; 1 Cor. 5:6; Gal. 5:9), Jesus here uses it to illustrate the spreading of good.

Parables on the Kingdom's Value (Matt. 13:44-46)
The Hidden Treasure (Matt. 13:44). Jesus tells of a man who finds a treasure in a field. He values the treasure so highly that he sells all his possessions in order to gain enough money to buy the field and thus obtain the treasure. As the treasure is worth more to the man than all his possessions, the blessings of God's kingdom are of greater value than all our earthly goods.

The Pearl of Great Price (Matt. 13:45-46). A merchant man is seeking valuable pearls when he finds one pearl of great price. The merchant sells all that he has in order to buy that one pearl. One who is searching for that which is of true value will give up everything for the blessings of the kingdom of God.

Questions

1. Men are brought into submission to King Jesus through the sowing of seed. True or False_____

2. When seed is sown, it works through a gradual, invisible process to produce the blade or stem, then the _____, and finally seed filling the ear.

3. When the word is sown in a man's heart, we cannot see the word working within him, but what can we see? _____
   _____

4. When Jesus began his reign, what could have discouraged the disciples?
   _____

5. From the tiny mustard seed, there grew a plant so large that what creatures could make use of it? _____

6. Leaven is always used in the Bible to illustrate the spreading of evil. True or False _____

7. By what means would the kingdom spread? _____
   _____

8. In the book of Acts we read of the growth of the kingdom. In Jerusalem,

3,000 submitted to King Jesus on Pentecost (Acts 2:41). How often were more added to this group (Acts 2:47)? _____

9. By the time Peter and John were arrested, how many men (males) had put their faith in Christ (Acts 4:4)? _____

10. As the apostles continued to do miracles in Jerusalem, _____ of men and women submitted to the King (Acts 5:14).

11. Saul led a great persecution against Christians in Jerusalem. How did this affect the growth of the kingdom beyond the city of Jerusalem (Acts 8:4)? _____

    _____

12. Herod killed James and arrested Peter. Did this deter the growth of the kingdom (Acts 12:24)? _____

13. What can you do to help the kingdom to continue its growth?_____

    _____

14. In the Parable of the Hidden Treasure, what did the man do when he found treasure hidden in a field? _____

    _____

15. In the Parable of the Pearl of Great Price, what did the merchant do when he found the pearl of great price? _____

    _____

16. Why are the blessings of the kingdom so valuable that you would give up anything to have them? _____

    _____

17. The man who found the treasure in the field was joyful as he gave up everything in order to obtain that treasure. What should your attitude be if you have to make some sacrifices to enjoy the blessings of the kingdom? _____

    _____

18. Jesus said that one who will not forsake all that he has cannot be his _____ (Luke 14:33).

19. If we have family members who are hostile toward the truth, we

may have to give up good relations with them. Jesus said that if we love father, mother, son, or daughter more than him, we are not _____ of him (Matt. 10:36-37).

20. We may have to give up some money (for example, if we have been obtaining it dishonorably). Jesus said that we should be laying up treasures in _____, not on _____ (Matt. 6:19-20).

21. The blessings of the kingdom include glorification in heaven, and that is worth more than whatever we may endure to obtain it; for "the _____ of this present time are not worthy to be compared with the _____ which shall be revealed in us" (Rom. 8:18).

The Unmerciful Servant

(Matt. 18:21-35)

Question Leading to the Parable (vv. 21-22)

Peter asks how often he should forgive a brother who repeatedly sins against him. Peter thinks he is being quite generous in suggesting that he should do so seven times.

Jesus replies that he should forgive not merely seven times, but seventy times seven. He obviously does not mean that one should forgive a literal 490 times, then stop. His point is that one does not keep count; he just continues to forgive. A Christian should have a loving, forgiving heart, and his heart does not change after he has extended forgiveness a certain number of times.

The Parable (vv. 23-34)

A king is settling the accounts of his servants, and one of them owes him ten thousand talents. This is an enormous sum of money. Fluctuating monetary values make it impossible to know the exact value of ten thousand talents in dollars, but it would be in the millions. Not surprisingly, the servant is unable to pay this staggering debt.

In keeping with laws and customs of the time, the king commands that the servant, his wife, his children, and his possessions be sold. The sale will not bring enough to pay the debt, but it is the only way for the king to get even a small portion of what the servant owes him.

The servant falls down before the king and begs him to have patience. He promises to pay him all he owes — a promise the king knows the servant will never be able to keep. The king is moved with compassion and does more than the servant asks. He does not merely give him more time to pay the debt; he *forgives* him the debt. This means that it is as though the debt was never incurred. The obligation to pay it is removed.

That servant then goes out and finds a fellow servant who owes him a small debt. The debt of 100 pence (*denarii*) is but a tiny fraction (one six-hundred thousandth) of the debt of which the king has forgiven him. This servant takes his fellow servant by the throat and demands payment. The fellow servant falls down at his feet and begs for patience, promising to pay all the debt.

The servant, however, has no mercy on his fellow servant. This one to whom great mercy has been shown, the one who has been forgiven such a tremendous debt, refuses to have any mercy on his fellow servant. He casts the fellow servant into prison.

When other servants see his unmerciful action, they report it to the king. Understandably, the king is angry. He has mercifully forgiven this servant of a tremendous debt, but this servant has refused to forgive his fellow servant of a far smaller debt. The king, therefore, delivers him to tormentors until he pays all that he owes — which, of course, he could never do.

Application (v. 35)

After God has forgiven us of our sins against him, his wrath will bring punishment upon us if we fail to forgive our brethren who sin against us. It was despicable for the servant who had been forgiven such a great debt to extend no mercy to his fellow servant. Similarly, it is despicable for those of us whom God has so mercifully forgiven to extend no forgiveness to our fellow servants.

Should Forgiveness Be Conditional?

Jesus makes it conditional, saying "if he repent, forgive him" (Luke 17:3-4). Passages requiring a Christian to forgive his brethren must be viewed in the light of that principle. The Christian's forgiveness is modeled after God's (Eph. 4:32); and God does not forgive unconditionally (Acts 2:38; 8:22).

This does *not* mean that if a brother is unrepentant, one may harbor bitterness toward him or desire revenge against him. The Christian continues to love him and desires his well-being (just as God loves us before we meet his conditions to be forgiven). Nevertheless, he considers him to be guilty of the sin (just as God considers a person to be guilty of sin before he meets God's conditions for forgiveness).

Questions

1. Peter asked about the number of times one should _____ his brother.

2. One should keep count of the number of times he has forgiven a brother so that he will know not to forgive him on the 491st time. True or False

    _____

3. How much did the servant owe his king? _____

4. How was the king going to get as much payment as possible? _____

    _____

5. The servant begged the king to (a) be patient until he paid (b) forgive him the debt. (Underline your answer)

6. The king had compassion on the servant and (a) gave him more time to pay (b) forgave him the debt. (Underline your answer)

7. How much did the servant's fellow servant owe him? _____

8. When the fellow servant asked him to be patient with him, what did the servant do? _____

9. How did the king find out about the servant's unmerciful act? _____

    _____

10. The king thought that the servant should have had compassion on his fellow servant, just as the king had shown pity toward him. True or False

11. The king delivered the servant to the _____ .

12. Jesus said, "So likewise shall my _____ _____ do also unto you, if ye from your _____ forgive not every one his brother their trespasses."

13. What did James say about one who shows no mercy (Jas. 2:13)? ___

    _____

    _____

14. Jesus taught us to pray, "And forgive us our _____, as we forgive our _____" (Matt. 6:12). Then he said, "For if ye forgive men their _____, your heavenly Father will

also forgive you: But if ye forgive not men their _____,
neither will your Father forgive your _____."

15. Jesus said, "If he _____ forgive him" (Luke 17:3-4).

16. Does the instruction in Matthew 18:15-17 indicate that you are to forgive a brother who is unrepentant? _____

17. Paul said to be _____ and _____, forgiving one another as _____ for _____ sake has forgiven us (Eph. 4:32).

18. God's forgiveness is conditional. True or False _____

19. Does the fact that you have not forgiven one who sins against you necessarily mean that you are bitter toward him and desire revenge?

_____

_____

The Good Samaritan
(Luke 10:25-37)

Background of the Parable (vv. 25-29)

A lawyer asks Jesus a question. A "lawyer" is one who is learned in the Law of Moses and responsible for teaching it. Lawyers are also called "scribes." This lawyer asks Jesus what to do to inherit eternal life. The question is not a sincere effort to learn truth; its purpose is to test Jesus.

Fully aware of the lawyer's knowledge as well as his motive, Jesus replies by asking him what the Law says on the subject. The lawyer responds by quoting two commands that encompass all other commands of the Law: (1) love God with all your being, and (2) love your neighbor as yourself. Jesus commends his answer as correct.

The lawyer, however, feels the need for a further question in order to justify himself. In view of the obligation to love our neighbor, he asks, "And who is my neighbor?" This is the same as asking, "Whom am I obligated to love?" This question reflects the concept that certain people fit into the category of "neighbor," and I must love them but no one else. The lawyer's question is an effort to justify himself (v. 29). Jesus said to obey the command to love his neighbor (v. 28), so maybe he wants to justify his failure to love some on the grounds that not everyone fits the definition of neighbor.

The Jews had various ideas regarding the question, "Who is my neighbor?" They generally would include only Israelites. Many Pharisees would include only Pharisees. The scribes and Pharisees taught a doctrine that excluded their enemies. They taught, "Love your neighbor and hate your enemies" (Matt. 5:20, 43). This was obviously contrary to the Law of Moses, which teaches men to perform loving acts for their enemies (Exod. 23:4; Prov. 25:21).

Now the lawyer wants Jesus to define the word "neighbor" so as to show who fits into that category. Whom are we obligated to love? Jesus refuses to give such a definition of the term "neighbor." Instead, he gives the Parable of the Good Samaritan.

The Parable (vv. 30-35)

A man goes down from Jerusalem to Jericho and falls among thieves. To say that he goes "down" from Jerusalem to Jericho is an accurate description of the journey. The 17-mile road descends about 3400 feet between those cities. To depict the man falling among thieves on that road is realistic. The steep winding road passes through rugged, rocky, mountainous territory with caves and ravines that provide plenty of hiding places for the thieves that infest it. Thieves strip the man, wound him, and leave him half dead beside the road.

A priest comes that way. This, too, is realistic, for many priests live in Jericho and travel that road as they return home after the completion of their priestly duties in Jerusalem. The priest, however, simply passes by. He no doubt is diligent in many of the rituals of the Law, but he has no compassion on the man.

A Levite then comes that way. Levites are assistants to the priests as they perform their duties in the temple. The Levite, however, has no compassion on the thieves' victim. He continues on his way.

Finally, a Samaritan comes by. The Jews despise Samaritans (cf. John 4:9), but the Samaritan's actions put the priest and the Levite to shame. Unlike those two religious leaders, the Samaritan has compassion on the man. He treats his wounds with oil and wine (common treatment at that time), puts the man on his (the Samaritan's) beast, and takes him to an inn. There he takes care of the man. Before leaving the next day, he leaves payment to the innkeeper, asking the innkeeper to take care of the man. He promises that if the cost is greater than the two pence he left, he will pay it when he returns.

Application (vv. 36-37)

Following the parable, Jesus asks the lawyer to tell him which one of the three men is a neighbor to the one who fell among the thieves. The lawyer replies, "He that showed mercy on him." Jesus says, "Go, and do thou likewise."

Jesus is making the point that one is not to concern himself with the question of who is his neighbor (that is, whom is he obligated to love); rather, like the good Samaritan, he is to *be a neighbor* to all who need his neighborly assistance. The correct question is not, "Who is my neighbor?" The correct question is, "Am I being a neighbor?"

Questions

1. What is the lawyer's first question and why did he ask it? _____

   _____

2. Did the lawyer know the answer to his question? _____

3. What did Jesus say on another occasion about the two commands the lawyer quotes (Matt. 22:40)? _____

   _____

4. What is the lawyer's second question? _____

   _____

5. The question the lawyer asked is the same as asking, "Whom am I obligated to love?" True or False _____

6. The scribes and Pharisees taught the Law of Moses, which said to love your neighbor and hate your enemies. True or False _____

7. After giving a definition of the word "neighbor," Jesus gave the Parable of the Good Samaritan. True or False _____

8. The man who fell among thieves was traveling from _____ to _____ on a road that dropped _____ feet over a distance of _____ miles.

9. What did the thieves do to the man besides robbing him? _____

   _____

10. Who were the first two people who came by and saw the thieves' victim? _____

11. Whereas the thieves had seriously injured the man, these two had done nothing to hurt him. Why, then, should they be criticized? _____

    _____

12. What do we learn from John 4:9 about the attitude of the Jews toward Samaritans? _____

    _____

13. What quality of heart set the Samaritan apart from the priest and Levite?

    _____

14. "Blessed are the _____" (Matt. 5:7).

15. God desired _____ rather than mere sacrifices (Hos. 6:6).

16. God required his people to do _____, to love _____, and to walk _____ with God (Micah 6:8).

17. What kind of first aid did the Samaritan give the man? _____
    _____

18. How did he get the man to the inn? _____
    _____

19. How did he provide for the man to be cared for after he left the inn?
    _____
    _____

20. Is the Samaritan like those who will render help to their little circle of friends or family but no one else? _____

21. Following the parable, what question did Jesus ask the lawyer? ___
    _____
    _____

22. After the lawyer answered, what did Jesus say?_____
    _____

23. When one asks, "Who is my neighbor?" is he taking the right approach? _____

24. Paul said that as we have _____, we are to do good to _____ men, especially those of the household of _____ (Gal. 6:10).

25. Is physical need the only kind of need that should stir feelings of compassion and the desire to help (Matt. 9:36)?_____
    _____

Two Parables on Prayer

Luke is the writer who records both of our Lord's parables on prayer. This is interesting in view of Luke's greater emphasis on the prayer life of Jesus. Luke is the only writer who mentions Jesus' praying (1) when the Holy Spirit descended on him (3:21), (2) before choosing the twelve apostles (6:12-13), (3) at Caesarea Philippi before eliciting Peter's confession that he was the Christ, the Son of God (9.18), and (4) on the Mount of Transfiguration (9:28).

The Friend at Midnight (Luke 11:5-13)

Jesus tells of a man whose friend comes to his house at midnight asking for three loaves. The friend needs the food because a traveling friend has come to his house and he has nothing to feed him.

To get out of bed, trying not to disturb his children, and remove the heavy bar from the door to give bread to his friend would be a chore. The man, seemingly a little selfish, does not want to be imposed on. Yet, while his friendship with the petitioner does not motivate him to grant the request, his friend's importunity (shameless persistence) prevails.

The point is that if a selfish man will finally respond to a friend's request just to get rid of him, surely a loving, unselfish God will respond to the petitions of his children. If a man who *resents* a friend's request eventually responds, our Father, who *desires* our prayers, will certainly respond.

In verses 9-13 Jesus encourages his disciples to ask, seek, and knock. God will respond to our prayers as an earthly father responds to his son's requests. If men know how to give good gifts to our children, God surely knows how to give good gifts to his children.

In making this point, Jesus mentions one good gift in particular: the Holy Spirit. The Jews of Jesus' day were anticipating wonderful blessings. Their prophets had spoken of a kingdom that was to come, and Jesus had taught them to pray for that (v. 2). In connection with the coming of the kingdom, God would send an outpouring of the Holy Spirit (Joel 2:28-29; Acts 2:16-18). Hence, as they prayed for the coming of the kingdom, it was also appropriate for them to pray for the Holy Spirit to come. The two things were bound up together.

Though Jesus mentions one good gift (the Holy Spirit) as an example, the principle regarding prayer is applicable to whatever good gifts one may request (Matt. 7:11). God's promise to grant what Christians ask, however, is conditional. Prayer must be offered in faith (James 1:5-8). Also, our request must be according to his will (1 John 5:14). What we ask for may not be good for us, just as is sometimes the case with an earthly son's requests. Moreover, what we ask may interfere with God's plans in a way of which we are unaware. We do not always know the reason our request is contrary to God's will, but we trust his wisdom.

The Importunate Widow (Luke 18:1-8)

A widow comes before an ungodly, unjust judge seeking justice against her adversary. The judge refuses to respond (probably because she has no bribe to offer him), but this importunate (shamelessly persistent) widow continues until he finally yields to her pleas simply to get rid of her. If a wicked judge would give her justice simply to get her to quit pestering him, our righteous God will surely give his people justice if we are persistent.

Luke states the lesson of this parable in verse 1: "that men ought always to pray, and not to faint." Jesus has been talking about his coming to judge the ungodly and reward his followers. Before his coming, his followers will endure much hardship and persecution. They will be tempted to faint, to desert him. Hence, the question: "when the Son of man cometh, shall he find faith on the earth?"(v. 8). Jesus is teaching that his followers must be persistent, continuing to pray in faith, trusting that eventually, justice will be done (v. 7). Though he may delay for a long time, he will finally act; and when he acts, he will do so speedily to punish his enemies and reward his saints (v. 8). We must not lose heart but continue to pray in faith.

Questions

1. This lessons notes _____ (how many) occasions on which Jesus prayed, but Luke was the only writer who mentioned it.

2. The one who came to his friend's house at midnight said, "_____, lend me _____ loaves."

3. The man in the house said that he could not give him any bread because he did not have any. True or False _____

4. Like the man in the parable, God does not want to grant our requests, but if we keep pestering him, he finally will. True or False_____

5. Jesus said, "_____, and it shall be given you; seek, and ye shall _____; _____ and it shall be opened unto you."

6. If a son asks bread of his father, his father will not give him a _____; if he asks for a fish, his father will not give him a _____; and if he asks for an _____, his father will not give him a scorpion.

7. Jesus said that earthly fathers do not know how to give good gifts to their sons. True or False _____

8. What specific gift from the Father did Jesus mention? _____

   _____

9. According to 1 John 3:22, what must we do in order to receive the things we ask for? _____

10. Peter said, "The eyes of the Lord are over the _____, and his _____ are open unto their prayers" (1 Pet. 3:12).

11. As James discussed asking for _____, he said to ask in

    _____.

12. A father who loves his child always grants his child's request. True or False _____

13. Did Paul pray for something that God did not grant (2 Cor. 12:7-9)?

    _____

14. What did Moses pray for that was contrary to God's will (Deut. 3:23-27)? _____

    _____

15. Suppose you ask God to do something and he sees best not to do it. Do you believe that God may still respond to your prayer by helping in other ways — perhaps even in ways you do not recognize? _____

16. Which do you believe: (a) asking in faith means you are always convinced that God will do exactly what you ask for, or (b) asking in faith

means that you believe God will respond to your prayer in whatever way his wisdom deems best? _____

17. With what attitude should God's children approach his throne (Heb. 4:15-16)? _____

_____

18. In the Parable of the Importunate Widow, the judge did not grant her plea because he thought she was wrong. True or False _____

19. The judge finally gave her justice so that she would quit badgering him. True or False_____

20. God's elect cry unto him day and _____, and when he finally comes to execute justice, he will act (a) slowly (b) speedily. (Underline your answer.)

21. Because we know that God will finally act to reward the righteous and punish his enemies, we ought always to _____ and never to

_____.

22. Jesus asked if he, when he comes, will find _____ on the earth.

23. What does 1 Thessalonians 5:17 teach us to do? _____

_____

The Rich Fool

(Luke 12:13-21)

Request Leading to the Parable (vv. 13-15)

A man in Jesus' audience speaks up and asks Jesus to help resolve a dispute between him and his brother about their inheritance. Seemingly uninterested in the spiritual matters of which Jesus has been speaking, this man's mind is absorbed with this earthly concern.

Jesus refuses to become involved in their dispute. The settling of such matters is not his mission. He recognizes a higher need to which he addresses himself: the problem of covetousness (greed). When there are disputes over material possessions, covetousness is usually involved.

To covet is not merely to desire something; all of us desire things. Nor is it, as some have mistakenly said, to desire something that belongs to another. One would never buy anything from someone else if he did not desire that which belonged to him. To covet is to desire *greedily*. It is not merely to desire; it is to desire too strongly. If you desire something to the point that you would sin to get it or that you cannot be content without it, then you are guilty of coveting.

In warning against covetousness, Jesus gets to the source of covetousness when he says, "For a man's life consisteth not in the abundance of the things which he possesseth." Possessing things will not bring fulfillment and happiness to our lives. A failure to understand that principle results in covetousness.

The Parable (vv. 16-20)

A rich man produces a bumper crop. His existing barns are not sufficient to contain the fruit of his labors, and he plans to build larger barns in which to store his grain. It must be with a feeling of immense satisfaction that he says, "And I will say to my soul, Soul, thou hast much goods laid up for many years; take thine ease, eat, drink, and be merry."

Just as he is joyously planning his retirement to a life of leisure, however, God says, "Thou fool, this night thy soul shall be required of thee: then whose shall those things be, which thou hast provided?"

Closing Comment (v. 21)
"So is he that layeth up treasure for himself, and is not rich toward God." The reason this man is a fool is not that he is prosperous; it is that he is "not rich toward God." When he dies, all his earthly wealth is worthless to him. All that matters then is whether or not he is prepared to face God's judgment. Anyone, therefore, who neglects his responsibility to God is foolish.

Questions

1. A man asks Jesus to speak to his _____ so that he will divide the _____.

2. Jesus asks, "Man, who made me a _____ or a _____ over you?"

3. This man's request serves as an occasion to warn against the sin of _____.

4. If you desire another person's property and make him an offer to buy it, are you necessarily guilty of covetousness? _____

5. Money or other material things can mean so much to us that they become gods to us; hence, Paul described covetousness as _____ (Col. 3:5; Eph. 5:5).

6. Jesus said that one cannot serve both God and _____ (money) (Matt. 6:24).

7. Covetousness (the love of money) is a root sin; that is, it leads to many other evils (1 Tim. 6:9-10). List some of the things covetousness leads people to do in order to get what they want. _____

   _____

   _____

   _____

8. If you gamble with your neighbor, you are seeking to take his possessions, even though he does not want to give them up, without giving him anything in return. Is this an act of covetousness? _____
   Would love for your neighbor prevent such an effort to take his possessions? _____

9. We live in a prosperous society in which we see our friends and neighbors enjoying many nice things. How can our observance of their possessions affect our attitude? _____
   _____
   _____

10. Solomon learned that fulfillment and happiness do not come through material possessions. After describing his great wealth (Eccl. 2:4-10), he concludes that "all was _____ and vexation of spirit, and there was no _____ under the sun" (v. 11).

11. Rather than being covetous, we are to be _____ (Heb. 13:5).

12. Does being content mean (a) that we have absolutely no desire to have anything more than we already have, or (b) that we remain happy regardless of whether or not we are able to obtain some of the things we would like? _____

13. Paul realized that his material circumstances were relatively unimportant; hence, he had learned to be _____ regardless of his material state (Phil. 4:11-12).

14. In the parable, what did the rich man decide he needed to do because of the abundance of his harvest? _____
    _____

15. What would the rich man have done with some of his prosperity if he had been rich toward God (Eph. 4:28; 1 Tim. 6:17-19)? _____
    _____

16. How will covetousness affect one's giving to the work of the church? _____
    _____

17. What word in 2 Corinthians 9:7 describes the manner in which a covet-
    ous man gives? _____

18. God called the rich man a fool. In view of his accomplishments, how
    do you think his neighbors would have regarded him? _____

    _____

19. The rich man's possessions would be of no use to him when he died,
    "for we brought _____ into this world, and it is certain we
    can carry _____ out" (1 Tim. 6:7).

20. Emphasizing the temporary nature of earthly possessions, Jesus said
    not to lay up treasures on _____ where _____ and
    rust corrupt and where _____ break through and steal
    (Matt. 6:19).

21. To what did James compare the earthly glory of the rich man (Jas.
    1:10-11)? _____

    _____

22. Two men die. One is the man described in this parable — a man of
    great wealth. The other is a prisoner with hardly any earthly goods.
    One leaves all his wealth behind him when he dies. The prisoner has
    great wealth awaiting him — wealth that he will never lose — for he
    has laid up treasures in heaven. He views his death with joyful hope,
    saying, "Henceforth, there is laid up for me a _____ of
    _____, which the _____, the righteous
    judge, shall give me at that day" (2 Tim. 4:8).

Two Parables Concerning Repentance

The Fig Tree (Luke 13:6-9)

This parable must be considered in the light of its background (Luke 13:1-5). Some Jews in Jesus' audience mention certain Galileans whom Pilate slew while they were offering sacrifices. These Jews think that the Galileans suffered this fate because they were worse sinners than others. Jesus corrects this false idea, warning his audience that they too will perish if they do not repent. Jesus then speaks of eighteen people who were killed when the tower of Siloam fell on them. The reason for their fate is not that they were greater sinners than others in Jerusalem. Jesus again warns his audience that if they do not repent, they too will perish. The Jewish nation is to be destroyed.

Having thus warned the people to repent, Jesus emphasizes the need for repentance by telling this parable. A man has a fig tree in his vineyard, but when he comes seeking fruit on it, there is none. He tells the dresser of his vineyard that he has been seeking fruit on that tree for three years and has found none. He instructs the dresser of the vineyard to cut down the useless tree. The dresser of the vineyard, however, asks the owner to spare the fig tree for one more year while he makes every possible effort to get it to produce fruit.

Like the fig tree, the Jewish nation deserves destruction. Nevertheless, like the fig tree, the nation is spared for a while as God gives them opportunity to produce the fruits of repentance. Having warned the Jews that they must either repent or perish, Jesus shows that God is mercifully sparing them to give them the opportunity to repent.

Two Sons (Matt. 21:28-32)

In a discussion with some of the Jewish leadership, Jesus tells of a man who has two sons. He tells the first one to go work in his vineyard, but the son says, "I will not." Later, however, the son repents and goes. The man tells the second son to go work in the vineyard, and this son promises to do so; yet, he does not. Having set forth these facts, Jesus asks the Jewish leaders which of the two sons did the will of his father. They give the obvious answer: the first son.

Jesus then makes the application. The publicans and harlots, whom these Jewish leaders despise, are like the first son. They have been openly rebellious, saying "I will not" to the heavenly Father's commands, but they have believed the preaching of John the Baptist and repented. They, therefore, will enter the kingdom of God. These Jewish leaders, however, are like the second son. They claim to be obedient to God, but they are disobedient and unrepentant.

Questions

1. What false idea did Jesus correct regarding the slaying of certain Galileans? _____

2. What would the Jews have to do to avoid a fate similar to that of those Galileans? _____

3. What other incident did Jesus mention to make the same point? ___

    _____

    _____

4. Repentance is a change of mind. To repent of sin involves a determination to quit sinning. What causes this change of heart (2 Cor. 7:10)?

    _____

    _____

5. Give some verses in Acts that show that one must repent in order to avoid punishment for his sins._____

6. In the Parable of the Fig Tree, did the owner decide to cut the tree down the first time he found it fruitless? _____

7. The dresser of the vineyard was glad to cut that useless tree and get it out of the way. True or False _____

8. God is not slack in carrying out his promises to punish; rather, he is _____, not wanting any to perish but all to come to _____ (2 Pet. 3:9).

9. To whom was Jesus speaking when he told the Parable of the Two Sons (Matt. 21:23)? _____

10. If you heard both sons reply to their father's command, which one would you think was the obedient one? _____

11. The _____ son represents the Jewish leaders, and the other son represents the _____ and _____.

12. Into what would the publicans and harlots enter? _____

_____

13. The Jewish leaders had failed to believe _____ when he preached the way of righteousness.

14. John the Baptist had called on men to _____ because the kingdom of heaven was at hand (Matt. 3:2).

15. John demanded that men bring forth _____ that showed repentance (Matt. 3:8).

16. Which verse in the Parable of the Two Sons shows that the first son's repentance produced a change of action? _____

17. If one does not bring forth fruits of repentance, John likens him to a _____ that does not produce good fruit; it is cut down and cast the _____ (Matt. 3:8-10).

18. In light of the scriptures cited in answer to question number 5, will a thief be forgiven of his sins if he continues to steal? _____ A liar if he continues to lie? _____ An adulterer if he continues to live in an adulterous relationship? _____

19. Jesus on one occasion pointed out that the men of _____ had _____ at the preaching of _____, while the Jews of his generation had failed to repent at the preaching of one who was far greater (Matt. 12:41).

20. Whom does God command to repent (Acts 17:30-31)? _____

_____

Lesson 9

The Great Supper

(Luke 14:15-24)

Background of the Parable

Jesus is a guest eating in the home of one of the chief Pharisees. He has taught his fellow guests a lesson on humility and his host a lesson on respect of persons. Then one of the guests says, "Blessed is he that shall eat bread in the kingdom of God." The Jews picture the kingdom as being ushered in by a great banquet. This guest views himself as one who surely will participate in that blessing. Jesus, however, gives a parable designed to teach that many Jews who expect to enjoy the blessings of the kingdom will not do so.

The Parable

1. The Invitation. A man prepares a great supper and invites many. Later, when the time comes for the guests to come, the host sends his servant to inform them that the supper is ready. This was the customary practice. When a Jew invited guests to a feast, he first sent invitations telling them what day the feast would be served. Then when the day arrived and the feast was prepared, he sent a servant to those who had accepted the invitation, telling them that the time for the feast had arrived.

2. The Excuses. When the servant goes out to announce that the feast is ready, those who have accepted the invitation make excuses not to come. These are clearly just excuses, not reasons. These men simply do not want to go to the supper.

One says that he cannot come because he has bought a piece of ground and has to go see it. Are we to suppose that he bought it sight unseen and that there was no time he could see it except during this supper?

Another says he has bought five yoke of oxen and is going to test them. Are we to believe that he bought oxen that were untested and that there was no other time he could test them than during this supper?

Another says that he cannot come because he has gotten married. Does getting married mean an end to one's social life? Could he not have said, "I have recently married. Is it okay to bring my wife with me?"

3. The Host's Response. When the host learns of their excuses, he sends the servant out to find others — first those in the streets and lanes of the city, then those in the highways and hedges. He instructs the servant to "compel" those in the highways and hedges, for the servant will have to persuade them that people of their class are wanted at such a feast.

The Application

The blessings of the kingdom are compared to a feast. Inasmuch as the kingdom is spiritual, the blessings are spiritual (forgiveness of sins, fellowship with God, the hope of heaven, and ultimately, the fulfillment of that hope). For centuries, the prophets had told the Jews that the kingdom was coming but had not clearly explained its spiritual nature.

The Pharisees, like those with whom Jesus was eating, were confident that they would enjoy all the blessings of the kingdom. Yet, when the time came to enter the kingdom and partake of its spiritual blessings, they declined. Through John the Baptist, Jesus, the apostles working under the "limited commission," and the seventy disciples whom Jesus sent out, God informed them that the feast was at hand. Yet, they rejected those servants. Then when the apostles began on Pentecost to proclaim that the rule of Christ had begun, the Pharisees (generally) refused to submit to him and receive the blessings of his kingdom.

The invitation was extended to those whom the Pharisees held in contempt, including Gentiles, and many accepted. Perhaps those in the streets and lanes (v. 21) represent Jewish publicans and sinners, while those in the highways and hedges (v. 23) represent Gentiles. These would participate in the kingdom's blessings while the proud Pharisees would be excluded. This parable shows the extensiveness of the Lord's invitation. He wants all to come to his feast.

Questions

1. Where was Jesus when he spoke this parable? _____

2. Do you think this guest was thinking of a spiritual kingdom? _____

    _____

3. Did this guest understand the true nature of the kingdom?_____

4. In view of the persecutions, hardships, responsibilities, and restrictions
    on conduct that would characterize citizenship in the kingdom, why
    would Jesus describe the kingdom as a great supper — a *joyful* occa-
    sion (see Phil. 4:4; 1 Pet. 1:6-9; Matt. 5:10-12)? _____

    _____

5. When the feast was ready, what did the host do? _____

    _____

6. Only one of the excuses for not attending the feast was legitimate.
    True or False _____

7. Whom does the host represent?_____
    The excuse makers? _____

8. Those who made excuses to avoid going to the feast did not place a
    high value on the feast. Why do many people not properly value the
    blessings of the kingdom? _____

    _____

9. What two parables depict those who are wise enough to discern the
    value of the kingdom? _____

10. What emotion did the host experience when the servant told him of
    the excuses?_____

    _____

11. The host sent the servant into the streets and lanes of the city to bring
    in the poor, maimed, halt, and blind. True or False _____

12. After returning from the streets and lanes of the city, the servant reported
    that enough people had come to fill the house. True or False _____

13. The host told his servant to "compel" people to come in. By what
    compelling force are men brought into the kingdom (cf. Rom. 1:16;

John 6:44-45; Acts 2:37, 41; 18:8)? _____

_____

14. 2 Thessalonians 2:14 shows the means by which one is invited to the feast: He is _____ by the _____.

15. Study the following verses: Titus 2:11; 1 Timothy 2:4, 6; Mark 16:15; 1 Corinthians 6:9-11; Romans 10:12; John 3:16. Tell which one teaches that:

    a. The gospel was to be preached to every creature. _____

    b. God wants all to be saved. _____

    c. Christ died for all men. _____

    d. The grace that brings salvation is for all. _____

    e. There is no difference between Jews and Gentiles. _____

    f. God loves the whole world and gave his Son to save it. _____

    g. Even the lowliest of sinners may turn to Christ and partake of the spiritual feast._____

16. In view of God's desire for men to come to his feast, what should Christians be doing? _____

17. When someone rejects the gospel and says it is because there are hypocrites in the church, do you believe: (a) this is the real reason or (b) this is an excuse for someone who does not want to accept the Lord's invitation and is delighted that there are hypocrites to give him an excuse?

_____

18. Is there any valid reason to decline the invitation to our Lord's spiritual feast and go to hell for eternity? _____

_____

Lesson 10

Three Parables Depicting God's Concern for Sinners
(Luke 15)

Reason for the Parables (vv. 1-2)

Jesus gives his attention to publicans and sinners in his effort to turn them to God. The self-righteous Pharisees and scribes criticize him because he associates with such people, even to the point of eating with them. They should be delighted that Jesus is influencing these people to repent, but they have no love or concern for them, only disdain. Jesus tells the three parables of Luke 15 in response to this attitude. The parables emphasize that God loves the publicans and sinners, desires their salvation, and rejoices in their repentance.

The Lost Sheep (vv. 3-7)

A man having 100 sheep loses one of them. He is so concerned about the one that he leaves the 99 to go find it. Upon finding it, he joyfully puts it on his shoulders and carries it home. Then he calls together his friends and neighbors to rejoice with him.

The concern for the one sheep and the joy when it is found represents the concern God has for one lost sinner and the joy he feels when that sinner repents. God's attitude is opposite that of the scribes and Pharisees. They should have had concern for the publicans and sinners and should have rejoiced that these lost souls were coming to Jesus.

The Lost Coin (vv. 8-10)

A woman has ten coins. When she loses one coin, she lights a candle, sweeps the house, and searches diligently until she finds that coin. When she finds it, she calls her friends and neighbors to rejoice with her.

Her concern for the coin and joy upon finding it represents God's concern for one sinner and his joy when a sinner repents. This parable should have reinforced upon the scribes and Pharisees the lesson of the first parable. The shepherd obviously places a high value on the sheep and the woman places a high value on the coin. God values highly those for whom the scribes and Pharisees have only disdain.

The Lost Son (vv. 11-32)

A man has two sons. The younger son asks his father to give him his share of the inheritance, and his father complies. Shortly thereafter, this son takes his possessions and travels to a far country. There he wastes his money living an ungodly life. Men usually describe him as the "prodigal" (recklessly wasteful) son.

This son represents the sinner. As he desires independence from his father, so the sinner desires independence from God. This son obviously is not ready to be on his own. Physical sons should reach the point that they are ready to go out from their homes and make their own way, but no one is ever ready to be independent from God; we always need his guidance and help (Jer. 10:23). When men seek independence from God, they will bring upon themselves ruin just as this irresponsible young man did. When one forsakes God's wisdom, he will live as foolishly as this son did.

After the younger son has spent all he has, a famine arises. In order to sustain himself, he hires out to feed swine. To a Jew, for whom swine are unclean, nothing could be more degrading and humiliating. He even thinks he would like to eat the husks that the swine eat. Jesus depicts this young man as having sunk about as low as one could go. This description aptly symbolizes the spiritual condition of one who goes into sin.

The young man then "came to himself" (v. 17). He looks at his miserable circumstances and thinks of the nice home he left — where even the servants have more than enough to eat — and he comes to his senses. He realizes how foolishly he has acted. Men in sin need to "come to themselves," for they are not acting rationally. They need to take stock of their miserable spiritual condition and realize how foolishly they have behaved.

Then the young man determines to return to his father. He will go humbly, fully aware of his unworthiness, asking only to be treated as a servant rather than a son.

When the father sees him coming, he runs to him, falls on his neck, and kisses him. He instructs his servant to bring the best robe and put it on his son, and to put a ring on his hand and shoes on his feet. He says to kill the fatted calf that they might eat it and be merry. As the man rejoices when he finds the lost sheep and the woman rejoices when she finds the lost coin, the father rejoices at the return of his lost son. The father represents God. When a sinner returns to him, he receives him with joy.

The older brother is in the field. As he comes in he hears the merry- making and asks a servant the reason for it. The servant explains that his father is celebrating the return of the younger son. The older brother is angry. He views his younger brother with the kind of disdain that the scribes and Pharisees have for the publicans and sinners. As they criticize Jesus for receiving those lost souls, the older brother criticizes his father for receiving his younger brother.

When the older brother will not go in and join the celebration, the father comes out to him. The older brother self-righteously speaks of his own obedience and complains that his father has never provided such a feast for him and his friends. The father explains that the elder son has always been with him enjoying all the blessings of his home. Now that his lost brother has come home, it is fitting to celebrate his return.

Questions

1. Jesus spoke the parables of Luke 15 in response to whose criticism?

   _____

2. In the first parable, God's concern for the sinner is represented by a man's concern for one lost _____.

3. When the man found his sheep and when he called his friends and neighbors, what emotion was in his heart and what does it represent?

   _____

4. Who should have had that emotion in their hearts, but did not? ___

   _____

5. In the second parable, what shows the high value that the woman placed on the coin she lost? _____

6. If a brother in Christ falls into sin, how can we show that we value him as God does — both before he repents (Gal. 6:1) and after he repents (2 Cor. 2:7-8)? _____

7. In the third parable, what did the younger son ask for and receive?

   _____

   _____

8. What shows that he was not yet responsible enough to be on his own?

9. Are we ever ready to be independent from God? _____

10. When the famine arose in the far country, what was the young man forced to do in order to sustain himself? _____

11. What do his miserable physical circumstances symbolize? _____

12. When the young man "came to himself," what did he think of? ___

13. This son determined to go to his father, confess that he had _____ against heaven and that he was not worthy to be called his _____, and to ask to be treated as one of the hired _____.

14. In the son's decision, what two attitudes do we see that are necessary in order for a child of God to be forgiven (Jas. 4:10; Acts 8:22)? __

15. Will the heavenly father forgive a child of God who will not acknowledge his sinfulness (1 John 1:9)?_____

16. Did the son plan to offer an excuse for his behavior?_____

17. David said, "For I _____ my transgressions: and my _____ is ever before me" (Ps. 51:3).

18. What did the father do when he saw his son coming? _____

19. What four things did the father tell the servant to bring? _____

20. The father said, "My son was _____, and is alive again; he was _____, and is found."

21. What does the father's compassionate, joyful reception of his son represent? _____

22. Where was the older brother when the merrymaking began? _____

23. When the servant explained to him the reason for the celebration, what emotion did the older son feel? _____

    _____

24. Who is represented by the elder son? _____

25. What attitudes do you believe are reflected in the older son's statements of verses 29-30? _____

    _____

26. Of what fact did the father remind the son (v. 31)? _____

    _____

27. What did the father say was "meet" (fitting, appropriate)? _____

    _____

28. Which of the characters in this parable was Jonah most like (Jonah 1:2-3; 3:10-4:4)? _____

    _____

The Unjust Steward

(Luke 16:1-11)

The Parable

Verses 1-3 — The Steward's Problem. A steward is one who has been entrusted to manage the affairs or property of another. The steward in the parable is about to lose his position because of his unfaithfulness. His problem is how he will survive after his master puts him out.

Verses 4-7 — The Steward's Solution. He decides to make certain ones obligated to him so that they will receive him into their houses. Before losing his stewardship, he reduces the debts of those who owe his master. He tells them to cut their bills. His hope is that they will feel a sense of obligation to him and take him into their homes.

Verse 8 — His Lord's Reaction. The steward's lord commends him for his wisdom. The steward is shrewd with respect to attaining his worldly goals. The steward's lord is reacting much as we might when someone cheats us: Though we are angry, we might commend the person for his shrewdness. Perhaps the steward's lord is a rather worldly fellow himself so that he can especially appreciate such wisdom.

Jesus' Application (vv. 8-11)

Jesus says that children of this world (those whose hearts are set on earthly things) exercise greater wisdom in the pursuit of their material goals than children of light (disciples of Jesus) do in pursuit of our spiritual goals. We should set our minds on spiritual endeavors and exercise the same degree of wisdom in our spiritual pursuits that children of the world do in their material pursuits. As they devote their minds to their endeavors, we should devote our minds to such things as (1) learning how better to teach the lost, (2) avoiding being deceived by false teachers, (3) leading others out of error, (4) avoiding situations involving strong temptations, (5) teaching and training our children, (6) avoiding being a stumblingblock, (7) being of service to others, (8) not causing strife, (9) using our resources for good.

Jesus mentions in particular the wise use of money. He says that one should use the "mammon of unrighteousness" in such a way as to be given heavenly habitations. *Mammon* is an Aramaic word meaning money. The expression, "mammon of unrighteousness" (v. 9), is parallel with the expression "unrighteous mammon" in verse 11. The expression does not mean ill-gotten gain. Jesus is simply speaking of money, describing all money as unrighteous. How so? "Unrighteous mammon" is contrasted against "true riches" (v. 11). Spiritual riches are true; they are dependable and can be trusted. Earthly riches, however, are not "true"; they are undependable and deceitful (Matt. 13:22; 1 Tim. 6:17), hence "unrighteous."

As the steward used money to make friends who would receive him into their houses, we are to use money so as to be received into heavenly habitations. The friends who will receive us into Heaven include God, Christ, and the Holy Spirit, who will welcome us with open arms if we are faithful.

In saying that one should use money so as to be received into heavenly habitations, Jesus does not mean that one can buy his way into Heaven. Nevertheless, the manner in which one uses money is an indication of the faith and love in his heart. When one uses money to do good out of faith, love, and devotion to God, he is conducting himself in such a manner that he will be received into heavenly habitations (1 Tim. 6:17-19; Eph. 4:28: Heb. 13:16). Verses 10-12 stress the proper use of the earthly possessions with which one has been entrusted.

Questions

1. Of what was the steward accused? _____

    _____

2. When the steward knew he was going to lose his stewardship, what two methods of survival did he rule out? _____

    _____

3. When the steward called his lord's debtors, how much did he cut the debt of the one who owed oil? _____

    _____

4. Does the fact that his lord (master) commended his shrewdness mean that the steward's actions were right? _____

5. What does Jesus say about the children of this world? _____

    _____

6.   Why are followers of Christ called children of light? _____

_____

7.   What are some of the evils that result from one's failure to devote his mind to the exercise of wisdom in spiritual pursuits?_____

_____

_____

8.   Mammon means _____ .

9.   What word did Jesus use to describe mammon?   _____

10. The steward used money so as to be received into earthly houses. How is one to use money? _____

_____

11. If one uses his money to accomplish good, will he be received into heavenly habitations regardless of his conduct in other matters? __

12. Paul said to exhort the rich to do _____ and be rich in _____ works, thereby providing a good foundation for the time to come (1 Tim. 6:17-19).

13. What is one proper use of that which one earns (Eph. 4:28)?_____

_____

14. One is to do good and "communicate" (share), for God is pleased with such _____ (Heb. 13:16).

15. Christians should be generous enough to go to whatever extent necessary to care for the needy among us. To what extent did the Christians in Jerusalem go (Acts 4:34-35)? _____

_____

16. Christians in _____ gave generously, despite their own poverty, to help needy saints because they had first given _____ to the Lord (2 Cor. 8:1-5).

17. When the Philippians gave to Paul as he preached the gospel, that which they sent was a sweet-smelling _____ to God (Phil. 4:10-18).

18. It is proper for the preacher who has brought men _____ things

to receive _____things from them, for the Lord has or-
dained that those who _____ the gospel should _____
of the gospel (1 Cor. 9:11, 14).

The Rich Man and Lazarus

(Luke 16: 19-31)

Introduction

There has been considerable discussion as to whether this story is a parable or a historical account. It is true that the Bible does not call it a parable, but neither does the Bible call the story about the unjust steward a parable (Luke 16:1-8). In fact, Jesus uses the exact same words to introduce the story of the rich man and Lazarus as he does to introduce the Parable of the Unjust Steward: "There was a certain rich man" (vv. 1, 19).

Whether or not this story is a parable is really of no consequence. Some suggest that if it is a parable, then one cannot rely on what it teaches about life after death. This is not so. Jesus' parables depict realistic situations. If this is a parable, its description of life after death is just as true as the Parable of the Sower's description of what happens when seed is sown in various kinds of soil.

Jehovah's Witnesses deny that any part of man continues to live after the death of the body. This story refutes that error.

The Story

There is a rich man who lives in splendor. A beggar named Lazarus is laid at his gate, evidently by friends who put him there hoping that someone will provide help for him. The need for them to lay him at the gate indicates that he is unable to walk. The statement that he desires crumbs from the rich man's table indicates that if he receives any help, it is not a generous amount. To exacerbate his misery, scavenger dogs come and lick his sores.

The beggar dies and angels carry him to Abraham's bosom. This is a figurative way of describing his entering into a close relationship with Abraham. The rich man dies and is buried, surely with a grand funeral.

Following his death, the rich man is in "hell" and is in torment (v. 23). The Greek term rendered "hell" in the KJV is not the term that refers to the place of eternal punishment (*gehenna*). Rather, it is the term *hades*. Many Bible students hold the following view, with which I agree:

The term *hades* refers to the place where departed spirits go when the physical body dies. In hades, where these spirits await the final judgment, they receive a foretaste of their final destiny. Then at the final judgment, Christ will send them to their final abode — either Heaven or Hell (*gehenna*). The rich man is in that portion of hades reserved for the wicked. He is suffering torment while awaiting the final judgment when he will be sent to his final, eternal abode in Hell (*gehenna*). Lazarus, on the other hand, is in that portion of hades reserved for the godly, enjoying sweet fellowship with Abraham while awaiting the final judgment when he will be sent to his final, eternal abode in Heaven.

The rich man, suffering torment, sees Lazarus in Abraham's bosom. He cries out pleading for Abraham to send Lazarus to provide some relief (v. 24). Abraham, however, reminds him of his and Lazarus' contrasting circumstances while they lived on earth (v. 25). Furthermore, he says, there is a great gulf between them and no one from either side can cross it.

Then the rich man asks Abraham to send Lazarus back to testify to his five brothers so that they will be persuaded to change their lives and avoid going to the place of torment. Abraham refuses, pointing out that they have the testimony of Moses and the prophets; that is sufficient. The rich man thinks that if one goes to them from the dead, they will repent. Abraham, however, affirms that if they will not hear Moses and the prophets, they will not hear one who rises from the dead. Abraham's words serve as strong testimony to the power and value of Scripture.

Questions

1. Which is the better way to spend most of your time in this class period: (a) studying the story and the lessons it teaches, or (b) arguing over whether or not the story is a parable? _____

2. Even if the story is a parable, its description of life after death is true. True or False _____

3. Where was Lazarus laid and what did he desire? _____

   _____

4. Why was the rich man lost? _____

   _____

5. How can one be sure that Lazarus was not a lazy deadbeat undeserving
    of the rich man's help? _____

    _____

6. The _____ took Lazarus to a place where he enjoyed close
    fellowship with _____.

7. According to the view held by the writer of this workbook, were the
    rich man and Lazarus in their final, eternal abodes? _____

8. According to Acts 2:31, Jesus went to hades but did not remain there.
    By what word does Luke 23:43 describe the place he went on the day
    that he died? _____

9. When the rich man saw Lazarus in Abraham's bosom, what merciful
    act did he ask Abraham for? _____   _____

    _____

10. Of what fact did Abraham remind the rich man? _____

    _____

11. What existed between Lazarus and the rich man? _____

12. Is there any indication whether or not the rich man would receive a
    second chance after death and possibly join Lazarus in Abraham's
    bosom? _____

13. About whom was the rich man concerned? _____

    _____

14. Since Moses and the prophets had long been dead, how could Abraham
    say that the rich man's brothers had Moses and the prophets? ____

    _____

15. In that same sense could it be said that we have the New Testament
    apostles and prophets? _____

    _____

16. If the writings of Scripture do not persuade men to serve God, would
    a miraculous act do so? _____

    _____

17. John 11 tells of a different Lazarus being raised from the dead. Were

there those who knew of this, yet continued in their unbelief (John 11:45-46; 12:10-11)? _____

_____

18. What error taught by Jehovah's Witnesses does this story refute?

_____

_____

19. According to Matthew 10:28, what continues to live after men have killed the body? _____

_____

20. As Paul spoke of his death, he did not think he would cease to exist; he described his death as a _____ (2 Tim. 4:6).

21. What part of this story applies to "Spiritualism" (the belief that the dead communicate with the living)? _____

_____

The Pharisee and the Publican
(Luke 18:9-14)

Jesus speaks this parable to those who trust in their own righteousness and view others with disdain. The Pharisees are in this category, and a Pharisee is one of the two characters described in the parable. The other character is a publican. Both men go to the temple to pray, but there is no similarity between their prayers.

The Pharisee (vv. 11-12)

The Pharisee's prayer is described as being "with himself," perhaps indicating that God is not really involved; the prayer does not reach the divine throne. In his self-righteousness, the Pharisee thanks God that he is not like others, including the publican. He informs God of his own goodness, mentioning his fasting and his tithing. Fasting twice a week is not a requirement of the Law of Moses. In fact, the only set time for fasting is the annual Day of Atonement. The Pharisee does not ask for his sins to be forgiven, for he is unaware that he has any. Indeed, he trusts in himself that he is righteous (v. 9).

The Publican (v. 13)

Publicans were tax collectors, and their Jewish countrymen viewed them as the very lowest of sinners. Not only were they notorious for their dishonesty, but they were regarded as traitors because they collected taxes for the Romans, whose rule the Jews detested.

In stark contrast to the self-righteous Pharisee, the publican is keenly aware of his sinfulness. Too ashamed to lift his eyes toward Heaven, he smites his breast with strong feelings of remorse as he says, "God be merciful to me a sinner."

Self Exaltation Versus Humility (v. 14)

Following the two prayers, the publican is justified (declared innocent, not guilty) while the Pharisee remains unjustified. The one who exalts himself, as the Pharisee did, will be abased, but the one who humbles himself, as the publican did, will be exalted. Those who are too proud to recognize their sinfulness and seek forgiveness will remain guilty. Those who humbly recognize their sinfulness and seek divine mercy in accordance with God's teaching will be forgiven.

As Jesus begins describing the character of those who would receive the blessings of his kingdom, he says, "Blessed are the poor in spirit: for theirs is the kingdom of heaven" (Matt. 5:3). To be poor in spirit means to recognize one's spiritual poverty and the need for salvation. The publican was poor in spirit; the Pharisee was not. And his awareness of his sinfulness brought sorrow to his heart — an attitude God has always required (Joel 2:12-13; Jas. 4:9-10; 2 Cor. 7:10).

No one has the right to be like the self-righteous Pharisee. Every man must rely on divine grace, for all have sinned and have no hope apart from God's gracious forgiveness (Rom. 3:9-10; 23). Thus, every one is saved by grace and not because his works have been sufficient to earn his salvation (Eph. 2:8-9). Though one must meet conditions to be saved (Heb. 5:9), these conditions are not works that make one deserving of salvation; his salvation is still by grace (that is, undeserved).

To trust in one's own righteousness, as the Pharisee did, is a fatal error because all are guilty of unrighteous conduct. There are two conceivable ways by which one could be righteous: (1) live a perfectly righteous life — a feat that no one other than Jesus ever accomplished — and (2) be forgiven of one's unrighteousness. Because of one's failure to do the first, he must rely on the second.

Now that Jesus has died and his testament has become effective, one must meet the conditions set forth in that testament in order to have his sins forgiven. One who has not done so must have enough faith in Christ to repent of his sins (Acts 3:19), confess his faith (Rom. 10:9-10), and be baptized for the remission of sins (Acts 2:38; Mark 16:16; Acts 22:16). When he has done those things, he still deserves to be lost but God in his abundant grace forgives his sins. After he has entered into a union with Christ through being baptized into him (Gal. 3:27), he will still fall short of a sinless life. When he sins, he does not have to be baptized again; rather, he has the privilege of praying for forgiveness with a repentant heart (Acts 8:22).

Thus, although one fails to achieve righteousness on his own, those who — in the humble spirit of the publican — seek God's mercy on his terms can be justified. Praise God for his grace that is greater than our sins (Rom. 5:20).

Questions

1. To whom was this parable directed? _____

2. Since we are taught to offer thanks to God, the Pharisee is to be commended for his offering of thanks. True or False _____

3. According to the Sermon on the Mount, the Pharisee's fasting and other good deeds may have been for what purpose (Matt. 6:1, 5, 16)?

    _____

4. The Pharisee boasted that he gave tithes, but what did he probably lack (Matt. 23:23)? _____

5. If one has too high an opinion of his own righteousness, how will this affect the way he regards others? _____

6. For what two reasons did the Jews hold publicans in low esteem?

    _____

    _____

7. Name a publican who sought divine mercy and received it (Luke 19:1-10). _____

8. The publican was justified (declared innocent, not guilty) even though he had been guilty of sin. True or False _____

9. Those who humble themselves will be _____ and those who exalt themselves will be _____.

10. What beatitude describes the publican's recognition of his sinful, unworthy condition? _____

11. The same awareness characterized David, who said, "Have _____ upon me . . . For I acknowledge my _____: and my _____ is ever before me" (Ps. 51:1-3).

12. This awareness characterized the people on Pentecost, who were _____ in their _____ and asked what to do (Acts 2:37).

13. What passages indicate the need for the kind of sorrow that character-

ized the publican? _____

14. Paul showed that no one can depend simply on his own righteousness, affirming, "There is none _____, no, not one" and declaring that "all have _____ and come short of the _____ of _____" (Rom. 3:10; 23).

15. Paul was far from self-righteous because he was deeply aware of his dependence on God's mercy. He described himself as "_____ than the _____ of all saints" (Eph. 3:8) and as _____ of sinners (1 Tim. 1:15).

16. Does the fact that one is saved by grace mean (a) that he does not have to do anything to be saved, or (b) that nothing he does causes him to deserve salvation? _____

17. What did the Pharisee do that we do not have the right to do (Eph. 2:8-9)? _____

18. What are two conceivable means by which we could be righteous?

    _____

    _____

19. Give the conditions a non-Christian must meet to be forgiven of sins and at least one passage for each condition. _____

    _____

    _____

    _____

20. Think of the man who does not submit to the conditions for forgiveness, but he says, "I pay my debts, I am good to my family, I help my neighbor. I'm as good as anybody in the church and I'll get to Heaven as soon as any of those people do." Which character in the parable is this person more like? _____

    _____

    _____

The Laborers in the Vineyard
(Matt. 20:1-16)

Background of the Parable
(Matt. 19:27-30; Mark 10:28-31; Luke 18:28-30)

Jesus has just conversed with a rich young ruler who was unwilling to sacrifice his possessions (Matt. 19:21-22). Peter says, "Behold, we have forsaken all, and followed thee; what shall we therefore have?"

Jesus replies that during his rule, the apostles "shall sit on twelve thrones, judging the twelve tribes of Israel" (Matt. 19:28). We interpret this in light of New Testament teaching regarding the spiritual kingdom and the authority of the apostles. Jesus did not refer to literal thrones or to physical Israel. That the apostles would sit on thrones is a figurative way of describing the authority they exercise through their teachings. Physical Israel stands for the Lord's church, spiritual Israel.

Jesus proceeds to say that all who sacrifice to serve the Lord will enjoy blessings that far exceed whatever they give up (Matt. 19:29). Physical relatives are replaced by spiritual kin. Just as the relatives that one receives are spiritual, the "houses" and "land" that one receives stand for spiritual blessings. In addition to the abundant spiritual blessings in this life, the faithful will receive everlasting life in the world to come (Mark 10:29-30).

Having affirmed the blessings to come to those who make sacrifices to serve the Lord, Jesus responds to Peter's implication that greater service might earn a greater reward. He says that the first shall be last and the last, first. Then he illustrates what he means by relating the Parable of the Laborers in the Vineyard.

The Parable

A householder goes out early in the morning to hire laborers to work in his vineyard. He reaches an agreement with some to hire them for a "penny" a day. The term refers to the Roman *denarius*, which evidently was considered to be a fair wage for a day's labor.

The householder goes out into the marketplace about the third hour (around 9 a.m.), finds more unemployed men, and hires them to work. However, he does not agree to pay them a specific amount. He simply promises to pay them whatever is right. He does the same about the sixth hour (around noon), ninth hour (around 3 p.m.), and eleventh hour (around 5 p.m.).

At the end of the day, when it is time to pay his workers, the householder instructs his steward to begin with those who were hired at the eleventh hour. He pays each one a *denarius* — the amount he has agreed to pay those who worked all day. Naturally, when those who have worked only a little while receive a *denarius*, those who were hired first think that the householder will surely pay them more. Nevertheless, he pays them exactly what they have agreed on. They complain against the householder, "saying, These last have wrought but one hour, and thou hast made them equal unto us, which have borne the burden and heat of the day." Their attitude is understandable. I suspect that if I were standing in their place with sweat dripping from my weary body, I would be a little perturbed, too.

The householder points out that he has not wronged those who have worked through the day. He has paid them exactly what they agreed on. If he wants to be generous to the others, he has that right. When we consider the situation, we see that these men really are not complaining because he has paid them too little; they are complaining because he has paid the others more than they deserve. They are resentful of his generosity to the latecomers. One who looks on others with envy or jealousy is said to have an evil eye. The householder recognizes that these men are jealous of the mercy shown to the latecomers (v. 15).

The Lesson (v. 16)
"So the last shall be first, and the first last." This does not mean that the last will be rewarded and the first will not. All are rewarded in the parable, and they are rewarded equally. The early workers say, "and thou hast made them equal unto us" (v. 12), and the householder says, "I will give unto this last, even as unto thee" (v. 14). The point is, God does not distinguish between the first and the last. When God renders the final reward, it will not be on the basis of so much work for so much pay. By his generous grace, all who have faithfully labored in his vineyard will be rewarded.

Questions

1. What had the rich young man done after Jesus told him to give up his possessions? _____

2. Based on Peter's question, what do you think he may have believed about the reward for serving Christ?_____

    _____

3. The apostles would sit on _____ thrones.

4. For those who make sacrifices, how much greater than the sacrifices will their blessings be (Matt. 19:29)? _____

5. According to Mark's account, Jesus distinguished between what we receive "now in this _____" and what we receive "in the _____ _____ _____" (Mark 10:30).

6. After discussing the reward, Jesus said that the first would be _____ and the _____ would be first.

7. How many times did the householder go out and hire laborers? ___

8. The householder agreed to pay the first laborers he hired a penny (*denarius*) a day. True or False_____

9. He agreed to pay a penny (*denarius*) to those he later hired. True or False _____

10. At the end of the day, the first workers to receive pay were those who were hired about five p.m. True or False _____

11. The householder paid the same amount to all the workers. True or False _____

12. What did the ones who been hired early in the morning expect? ___

    _____

13. Those who had worked all day complained because some had worked but one hour, yet the householder had made them _____ to those who had labored through the day (v. 12).

14. On what basis did the householder contend that he had not wronged those who had labored all day (v. 13)? _____

    _____

15. On what basis did he defend his right to be merciful and generous toward the others (v. 15)? _____

_____

16. Were these men unhappy (a) because the householder had paid them too little or (b) because he had shown mercy to the latecomers? ___

_____

17. When God renders the final reward, it will not be based on rankings from first to last in service. True or False_____

18. Since God's reward is based on grace, not on so much work for so much pay, Christians do not have to work in order to receive the reward (cf. 1 Cor. 15:58; Gal. 5:6; Jas. 2:17-24). True or False_____

19. The work that we do in the Lord's vineyard is necessary as an expression of our faith, but it does not *earn* our eternal reward. True or False

_____

20. One who labors for many years in the service of Christ will receive the same eternal reward as the one who sincerely turns to Christ near the end of his life. True or False_____

21. Suppose you spend many years sacrificing to serve the Lord, then convert an old person nearing death. Would you resent that person receiving the same eternal reward you do? _____

21. Though the eternal rewards are equal, is the one who faithfully serves God throughout his life blessed in ways that the one who is converted late in life is not? _____

_____

The Parable of the Pounds
(Luke 19:11-27)

Reason for the Parable (v. 11)

Jesus and his disciples are traveling to Jerusalem for the last time. A few days after their arrival, Jesus will be crucified. The disciples, however, think that upon their arrival in Jerusalem, Jesus will begin his reign over a glorious earthly kingdom. In response to that expectation, Jesus relates the Parable of the Pounds (v. 11). The parable teaches them that they are not about to receive the kind of honor and glory they expect. Jesus will have to go away and return before defeating his enemies and rewarding his servants. In the meantime, they will have to serve patiently.

The Nobleman's Journey (v. 12)

The nobleman goes into a far country to receive his kingdom. Such is realistic. Herod the Great had willed that Archelaus succeed him as ruler over Judea, Samaria, and Idumea; but Archelaus had to go to Rome to have Herod's will confirmed and receive his kingship. The nobleman going to a far country to receive his kingdom symbolizes Christ's going to Heaven to receive his kingship (Acts 1:9-11; Dan. 7:13-14). He will not be crowned in Jerusalem as the people expect.

Jesus, having gone to the "far country" (Heaven), has received his kingdom and presently reigns (Acts 2:30-36; Heb. 1:3, 8; 1 Pet. 3:22; Phil. 2:8-11). His kingdom is a spiritual one, existing as he rules through the truth (his law) in the hearts of men (John 18:36-37; Luke 17:21). Those who submit to the king are delivered from sin and become citizens of his kingdom (Col. 1:13).

Gives Responsibility to Servants (v. 13)

The nobleman gives his ten servants ten pounds to use in his absence. Having shown that he will go away rather than set up a kingdom in Jerusalem, Jesus here shows that he expects faithful service during his absence.

It would be easy to worship and serve Jesus if he were visibly present in all his glory, but the test is whether one will serve him in his absence.

Rebellious Subjects (v. 14)

The citizens of the nobleman hate him and send a message saying that they will not have him to rule over them. This part of the story is realistic. When Archelaus was seeking to have his kingship confirmed in Rome, the Jews sent fifty messengers to Rome begging Caesar Augustus not to confirm his rule. In the parable, the refusal to submit to the nobleman's rule represents the refusal of many to submit to the rule of Christ.

Return to Judge (vv. 15-27)

The return of the nobleman from the far country (v. 15) represents Jesus' return from Heaven. Upon his return, the nobleman executes judgment.

First, he judges his servants according to their faithfulness (vv. 16-26). Those who have used the pounds that were entrusted to them are rewarded. One servant, however, is unfaithful. He has kept his pound in a napkin rather than using it. His excuse makes no sense. He claims that he fears the nobleman because he is a severe man who seeks to make gain through the labors of others. The nobleman responds that, if the servant views him in that way, the servant should have been all the more diligent to do what he could — even if it was just putting the money with money lenders who would pay some interest for it. The nobleman then orders that the unfaithful servant's pound be taken from him and given to the one who has gained ten pounds. The one who has gained through his diligent effort is rewarded. It is a fact of life that those who make gain through diligent use of their opportunities will make more gain, and those who do not will lose. Similarly, the diligent use of opportunities to produce spiritual fruit will be rewarded.

The nobleman then orders that his enemies (described in v. 14) be slain (v. 27). Those who reject the rule of Christ will suffer his wrath when he returns (2 Thess. 1:7-9).

Jesus has now gone into a "far country" (Heaven). When he returns, having received his kingdom, he will judge us on the basis of our conduct while he was away. There are three classes, and each of us is in one: (1) faithful servants, (2) those who have committed themselves to serve but are not faithful, and (3) enemies who reject his rule.

Questions

1. What did the disciples think was going to happen when they arrived in Jerusalem? _____

    _____

2. What would Jesus do before establishing his kingdom? _____

    _____

3. What would the disciples have to do before receiving their glorious reward from the King Jesus? _____

    _____

4. The nobleman's going to a far country to receive his kingdom is similar to Archelaus' going to _____ to receive his kingship.

5. Christ went to _____ to receive his kingdom, rather than being crowned in the city of _____ as his disciples expected.

6. When Jesus ascended, "an _____ received him out of their (the apostles') sight" (Acts 1:9), and when he entered Heaven, "there was given him _____, _____, and a _____ " (Dan. 7:13-14).

7. Give a verse proving that Jesus' kingdom is now in existence. _____

8. Explain the nature of his rule. _____

    _____

9. The nobleman expected his servants to use the pounds to make gain for him. What does this indicate about our Lord's expectations of us until he returns? _____

    _____

10. It was unrealistic to depict the subjects of the nobleman sending a message rejecting his rule. True or False _____

11. When people refuse to submit to any teaching of Jesus, whether it pertain to the husband's headship in the home, divorce and remarriage, or any other subject, they are saying in effect, "We will not have this man to _____ over us" (v. 14).

12. Like the nobleman, when Jesus returns he will _____ his servants and his enemies.

13. In the parable, one servant had gained _____ pounds and another had gained _____ pounds.

14. Do you believe (a) that the fact that these two servants received different rewards was simply a detail to make the story realistic, having no bearing on the point Jesus was trying to illustrate, or (b) that Jesus was seeking to illustrate the point that he will grant differing rewards in Heaven based on the differences in what we accomplish? (Don't forget Lesson 14.) _____

15. What did the unfaithful servant do with his pound? _____

_____

16. When men make excuses for their failures, their excuses often do not make sense. True or False _____

17. What was the least this unfaithful servant should have done? _____

_____

18. What did the nobleman order be done to his enemies? _____

_____

19. Christ will come in _____ fire, taking vengeance on those who _____ not God and obey not the _____ (2 Thess. 1:7-9).

20. What three classes of people, found in this parable, will Jesus judge when he returns? _____

_____

The Wicked Husbandmen
(Matt. 21:33-46; Mark 12:1-12; Luke 20:9-19)

Jesus is in Jerusalem during the week of his crucifixion. This is the second of three parables Jesus addresses to the Jewish leaders who are planning to kill him. The first was the Parable of Two Sons (Matt. 21:28-32; cf. Lesson 8).

The Householder and His Vineyard

A householder plants a vineyard and does everything possible for its protection and well-being. He hedges it (putting a plant hedge or a wall around it), makes a winepress in it, and builds a tower from which watchmen can watch for any approaching danger. Then he lets it out to husbandmen and goes into a far country. This involves leasing it to sharecroppers with the agreement that he will receive a certain portion of the vineyard's fruit.

The householder represents God and the vineyard represents Israel. God had lovingly built the nation of Israel and he had done all that was possible for her well-being. He had the right to expect the fruit of obedience from her (Isa. 5:1-2, 7).

The Householder Sends His Servants

When the time comes for the vineyard to bear fruit, the householder sends servants to the husbandmen to receive the portion of fruit that is due him. The wicked husbandmen, however, refuse to give the fruit that is due. Instead, they abuse the servants. The householder then sends more servants and the husbandmen respond to them in the same way.

Throughout Israel's history, God had sent servants (prophets) to Israel, calling on them to render to God the fruit of obedience. Time and again, however, Israel had failed to render to God the fruit that was due him, and their leaders had persecuted the prophets whom God sent to demand that fruit.

The Householder Sends His Son

The forbearing, longsuffering householder finally sends his son. He thinks that surely the husbandmen will respect his son. The husbandmen, however, plot to kill the son. They think that if they eliminate the heir to the vineyard, they will be able to claim it as their own. Hence, they cast him out of the vineyard and slay him.

The forbearing, longsuffering God sent his only Son to the Jewish nation. Throughout their history, the leadership had led the people to reject and persecute the servants he had sent. Now they rejected his Son and would kill him.

Discussion Following the Parable

After telling of the husbandmen's killing the householder's son, Jesus asks his audience what the householder will do to those husbandmen. The answer is obvious: He will destroy those wicked husbandmen and let out his vineyard to others.

Jesus then asks them if they have read the Scripture that says, "The stone which the builders rejected, the same is become the head of the corner." This Scripture is referred to a number of times in the New Testament (Acts 4:11; 1 Pet. 2:7). The Jewish leaders are like builders who reject a stone that later becomes the most important stone in the building. They should have been prominently involved in furthering the divine plan, but they rejected the one who has the supreme place in that plan. Their rejection of Jesus was a colossal blunder. This was the tragic error they were making when they killed the Son of God.

Jesus affirms that the kingdom will be taken from them and given to a nation producing good fruit. Under their leadership, the vineyard has not yielded good fruit to God. After years of abusing God's servants, they will now slay his Son. Hence, they will lose God's vineyard. The Israel that was under their leadership (physical Israel) would no longer be the kingdom of God. Another nation would enjoy that privilege — a nation consisting of those who would produce the fruit God seeks. That nation consists of Christians, those who submit to the teachings of Christ. These constitute a holy nation (1 Pet. 2:9). In Christ, Jews and Gentiles are reconciled to God in one body and are *fellow citizens* of our Lord's kingdom (Eph. 2:16, 19).

Jesus describes the terrible fate of those who reject him. He is like a stone that will pulverize that on which it falls.

The chief priests and Pharisees perceive that Jesus is referring to them. Yet, they are afraid to capture him because of the multitude.

Questions

1. At what point in Jesus' life did he tell this parable? _____

    _____

2. When the householder planted a vineyard, what three things did he do? _____

    _____

3. What arrangements pertaining to the vineyard did the householder make when he went into a far country? _____

    _____

4. Who is represented by the householder? ___ _____
    The vineyard? _____

5. Isaiah said, "For the _____ of the Lord of _____
    is the _____ of _____ " (Isa. 5:7).

6. When the householder sent servants to receive the portion of fruit that was due him, the husbandmen _____ one, _____
    another, and _____ another.

7. When the householder learned about the treatment of these servants, what did he do? _____

8. Whom do the servants represent? _____

9. Jesus lamented the fact that the Jews had _____ the prophets and _____ those who were sent to them (Matt. 23:37).

10. Stephen asked, "Which of the _____ have not your fathers _____ ?" (Acts 7:52).

11. Whom did the householder send last? _____

12. Why do you think Jesus is depicting the householder as being so patient and forbearing, rather than taking immediate vengeance on those who had slain his servants? _____

    _____

13. "But to Israel he saith, All day long I have stretched forth my _____
    unto a _____ and _____ people" (Rom. 10:21).

14. The householder expected the husbandmen to kill his son. True or False _____

15. At the conclusion of the parable, Jesus asked a question and received the correct answer. True or False _____

16. To illustrate the folly of their rejecting Jesus, to whom did Jesus compare the Jewish leaders? _____

17. The rejection of Jesus included killing him. Since he would be killed, what would be necessary before he could become the chief cornerstone?

    _____

18. The kingdom of God would be given to a _____ bringing forth the _____ thereof.

19. The church is now God's holy nation. True or False _____

20. Israel failed to produce the fruit God sought from his vineyard. What fruit does God seek from his people now (Gal. 5:22-23)? _____

    _____

21. The chief priests and Pharisees did not understand that Jesus was referring to them. True or False _____

22. Why did the Jewish leaders not immediately kill Jesus as they desired to do? _____

    _____

The Marriage Feast
(Matthew 22:1-14)

Introduction

Jesus is in Jerusalem during the last week of his life when he speaks this parable — the third in a series of parables in which he addresses the Jewish leaders who are planning to kill him. This parable is similar to the Parable of the Great Supper, which he has previously given; but Jesus delivers this parable on a different occasion, and it includes elements not found in that parable. We should not be surprised that Jesus uses similar stories to illustrate his points.

Rejection of Invitation (vv. 2-7)

A king gives a wedding feast for his son. When the time comes for the guests to come, he sends servants to call them; but they refuse to come. They have already been bidden (invited) and have evidently accepted the invitation. The Jewish custom was for the host to send invitations telling the day on which the feast would be served. Then when the day arrived and the feast was ready, he would send servants to those who had accepted the invitation, telling them that it was time to come to the feast.

The Jews had been bidden to God's feast (the blessings of the Messiah's kingdom), for through his prophets, God had told them about the kingdom. Now God had sent to them servants telling them that the time had come; the kingdom was soon to be established. He had given them this message through John the Baptist (Matt. 3:1-2), Jesus (Mark 1:14-15), the twelve under the "Limited Commission" (Matt. 10:5-7), and the seventy disciples (Luke 10). The Jewish leadership, however, rejected those servants. Later, after the kingdom began, the apostles delivered the news of its establishment first to the Jews, and many of the Jewish leaders rejected their message and refused to come to the feast.

The king in the parable is patient. Upon the first refusal, he sends more servants to urge those who were bidden to come (v. 4). Similarly, God was patient with the Jews, giving them ample opportunity.

The king's patience, however, does not bring the results he desires. Those who were invited respond to the servants in two ways:

1. Some are indifferent to the invitation, choosing to go about their normal business rather than attend the feast (v. 5). Indifferent to a feast given by a king? That is remarkable, but not as remarkable as the fact that some are indifferent to the marvelous blessings of the kingdom of Christ. There have always been those who are more interested in their earthly pursuits than in heavenly blessings.

2. Others treat the servants violently (v. 6). The Jewish leadership mistreated and abused the servants God sent to them. They crucified Jesus, and they persecuted the apostles and others who urged the Jews to come and partake of the blessings of the kingdom (John 16:2; Acts 4:1-3; 7:54-60).

The king's response to the violent treatment of his messengers is to destroy them and their city (v. 7). Similarly, God would destroy the city of Jerusalem (Matt. 23:37-38; 24:1-2; Luke 19:41-44).

The Invitation Enlarged (vv. 8-10)
The king says that those who were originally invited are not worthy. He sends his servants into the highways to invite as many people as they can find. The servants go to the highways and bring in as many as they find, both good and bad.

Similarly, the Jews who rejected the Lord's invitation were not worthy of the blessings of the kingdom; hence, the invitation was extended to the gentiles (Acts 13:44-46). The gospel is for all (Matt. 28:18-20; Mark 16:15; Rom. 1:16). It is for both good and bad (v. 10). Thus, it was extended to the good Cornelius (Acts 10) and to the immoral Corinthians (1 Cor. 6:9-11; cf. Matt. 21:32).

The Improperly Attired Guest (vv. 11-14)
The king finds one guest at the feast whose attire is not appropriate for a wedding. When the king questions him, he has no excuse. The king orders his servants to cast out the man.

The privilege of partaking of the divine feast carries with it the responsibility to dress appropriately. One is to put on godly qualities so that he will be properly clothed (Col. 3:12; Eph. 4:22-24). The man who has accepted the invitation, yet lives an ungodly life, is not properly arrayed. An improperly dressed guest at a king's feast would (1) detract from the splendor of the feast and (2) show a low regard for the occasion. One in the Lord's kingdom who is not attired in righteousness detracts from the kingdom's glory and demonstrates a low regard for the kingdom. Hence, many who are called will be rejected.

Questions

1. To whom was this parable addressed? _____

2. The king sent servants to call those who had already been invited to his son's marriage feast. True or False _____

3. Who had been invited to the blessings of the Messiah's kingdom?

_____

4. When the time came to partake of the kingdom's blessings, whom did God send to inform those who had been invited? _____

_____

5. The king in the parable showed no patience toward those who would not come? True or False _____

6. When the king sent more servants, those who had been invited received them in what two ways? _____

_____

7. What is even more remarkable than the fact that some were indifferent to the king's feast? _____

_____

8. What did Jesus say about those who would kill the apostles (John 16:2)? _____

9. Who arrested Peter and John (Acts 4:1-3)?_____

10. What action of Jewish leaders is recorded in Acts 7:54-60? _____

_____

11. The king's patience finally came to an end. True or False_____

12. In Matthew 24:1-2 Jesus predicted the destruction of the _____, which was in Jerusalem.

13. Why did Jesus weep in Luke 19:41-44? _____

14. The king said that those who had originally been invited to the feast were not _____ (v. 8); therefore, his servants were to go to the _____ and invite as many as they found.

15. When Paul and Barnabas preached in Antioch, the Jews who rejected the gospel put themselves into the category of those who were not worthy of_____; therefore, Paul and Barnabas turned to the _____ (Acts 13:46).

16. The king's servants went out to the highways and invited only good people to the feast. True or False _____

17. The gospel's invitation is for both Jews and Gentiles, and for both the good and the bad. True or False _____

18. Why did the king order a guest to be cast out of the marriage feast?

    _____

19. What is the proper attire for those who partake of the blessings of the kingdom? _____

20. When a Christian sina and thus blemishes his attire, is there a remedy (Acts 8:22; 1 John 1:9; 2:1)? _____

21. What will be his fate if he fails to avail himself of the remedy (v. 13)?

    _____

The Ten Virgins
(Matt. 25:1-13)

The Parable (Verses 1-12)

Excitement must be building as the time approaches for the wedding —
especially among the ten virgins who are to have a part in the festivities.
They will carry lights as they accompany the bridegroom in the procession
to the wedding feast. Five of these virgins wisely exercise the forethought
to take oil (olive oil) for their lamps.[1] The other five take no oil to burn. It
is easy to understand why the Lord describes them as foolish; the lamps
are worthless without oil.

For some reason the bridegroom tarries, and it is understandable that these
ladies fall asleep while they wait for him — though the foolish ones could
have better spent the time finding some oil. Finally someone cries out that
the bridegroom is coming. The virgins arise and prepare their lamps. When
they light them, however, the foolish virgins' lamps quickly go out. There
is a residue of oil that enables the girls to light the lamps, but not enough
to continue burning. As their lights flicker and go out, it finally occurs to
these five virgins that lamps require oil. They ask the five wise virgins to
give them some of theirs.

Understandably, the five wise virgins refuse. They have brought enough
for themselves but not enough for themselves and those who were too foolish to bring their own. They tell the five foolish virgins to go and buy some.
While the five foolish virgins are out looking for oil to buy, the bridegroom
comes. The five who are prepared go with him to the festivities. After they

---

[1] The term translated "lamps" is *lampas*, which was normally used to denote
a torch. Torches were fed with oil from small vessels designed for that purpose.
There is disagreement whether the term in this parable refers to a torch or a lamp.
Inasmuch as the term "lamp" is used in most translations, we will use that term in
our discussion of the parable. The point of the parable is not affected.

enter, the door is shut. Later, when the other virgins come, they seek admission but are refused.

Application (v. 13)

We do not know when Christ will come, and we must constantly watch — that is, remain prepared. This parable illustrates the folly of failing to be prepared for his coming. When he comes it will be too late to prepare, and if we are unprepared, the door to eternal glory will be tragically shut.

Questions

1. What role were the ten virgins to play in the wedding? _____

    _____

2. How much oil did the five foolish virgins take? _____

3. How many of the virgins slept while the bridegroom tarried? _____

    _____

4. When did the bridegroom come, and how did the virgins know of his approach? _____

5. When the foolish virgins' lamps went out, what did they try to do?

    _____

6. Why did the wise virgins refuse the request of the foolish virgins?

    _____

7. Where were the foolish virgins when the bridegroom came?_____

    _____

8. After the five wise virgins entered into the marriage feast, what was done? _____

9. When the five foolish virgins sought entrance to the feast, what were they told? _____

10. What is the main lesson of the parable? _____

    _____

11. This parable follows a series of warnings similar to that of verse 13. Jesus said "But of that _____ and hour knoweth no _____ " (24:36) . . . "_____ therefore: for ye know not what _____ your _____ doth come" (24:42). . . . "Therefore be ye also

_____: for in such an hour as ye _____ not the Son of man cometh" (24:44).

12. How did Peter say the day of the Lord will come (2 Pet. 3:10)? ___

_____

13. What did the Thessalonians know about the Lord's coming (1 Thess. 5:2)? _____

_____

14. When Paul told the Thessalonians that the day of the Lord would not "overtake" them as a thief, did he mean (a) that they would know when it would come or (b) that it would not catch them unprepared? ___

15. When speaking to one whom many men would consider to be wise, God said, "Thou _____" (Luke 12:20) because he was not prepared to face God.

16. One who does not obey Jesus, and is therefore unprepared for his judgment, is as foolish as one who builds his _____ on _____" (Matt. 7:24-27).

17. When Jesus condemned saying to someone, "Thou fool" (Matt. 5:21-22), was he referring to (a) calling someone a denigrating name out of bad feelings toward him, or (b) describing what his conduct proves him to be? _____

18. Can you think of a lesson to be learned from the fact that the five foolish virgins could not overcome their lack of preparation by getting oil from the others? _____

_____

19. What in the parable indicates the finality of one's fate when he is caught unprepared? _____

20. Will one have any opportunity to prepare after death (2 Cor. 5:10; Eccl. 9:10)?_____

21. To be prepared, one must be blameless and without spot (1 Thess. 5:23; 2 Pet. 3:14). Since all of us sin, how is it possible to be in that condition when Jesus comes? _____

Lesson 19

The Talents

(Matt. 25:14-30)

Servants Entrusted With Money (vv. 14-18)

A well-to-do man is traveling to a far country. Before leaving, he calls his servants and entrusts them with his possessions. To one he gives five talents, to another two, and to another one. A "talent" was a measure of weight and also an amount of money. The man does not want this money to lie idle during his absence, so he puts it into the hands of his servants, giving them the responsibility to use it to make a profit for him. He recognizes their varying business skills and distributes the money accordingly — that is, "to every man according to his several ability."

The servant who receives five talents uses the money well; he doubles that amount. Similarly, the one who receives two talents doubles that which he has been given. But the one who receives one talent fails to make any profit for his master. He simply buries the talent.

The man who was traveling represents Jesus. Jesus has departed this earth, and he has entrusted us with the work he wants done. Like the man in the parable, he expects us to be serving him during his absence. We are to be doing such things as teaching the gospel, setting a good example, and helping those in need. We can do as the two servants who made gain for their master, using our opportunities to accomplish good, or we can do as the one who made no gain, failing to use our opportunities.

The Reckoning (vv. 19-30)
The Faithful Servants

After a long time, the master returns and "reckons" (settles accounts) with the servants. He heartily commends the servants who have used their talents to make gain. He tells them that, because of their faithfulness in handling the responsibilities he has given them, he will reward them with even greater and more honorable realms of responsibility. The master invites them to enter into the joy of their lord; they will rejoice with him in celebration.

When our Lord returns, he will reward those who have faithfully served him. Note that the lord was as pleased with the one who had gained two talents as he was with the one who had gained five. The one who had gained only two had begun with only two; hence, he had not had the opportunity to make as much gain as the one who had been given five. God expects service commensurate with opportunity. One may be unable to teach verbally because of speech problems, but he may have opportunities to teach through giving away tracts. One may be able to pay a month's rent for a needy brother, while another may be able to do no more than buy him some groceries. We are responsible for using whatever opportunities we have, be they great or small.

The Unfaithful Servant

After the master has commended the faithful servants, the unfaithful servant comes to give account for himself. His excuse for burying his money is absurd. He says that he buried it because he was scared of his master! The servant claims that he knows his master is a hard man who profits from the labor of others, reaping where he has not sown. He fears losing the money of such a master, so he hides it in the ground to keep it safe. The master quotes the servant's own words to show the absurdity of his excuse. If the servant really knew that his master was such a harsh fellow, he ought to have exerted even more effort. If nothing else, he could have put it where it would have drawn interest. The master reveals the true reason for the servant's neglect when he calls him a "wicked and slothful servant."

The master orders that the one talent be taken from this servant and given to the one who has ten talents. This is in fulfillment of the principle that "unto everyone that hath shall be given, and he shall have abundance: but from him that hath not shall be taken away even that which he hath." The servant had ten talents because of his diligence in using his opportunity. It is a fact of life that such a course brings more gain. The other servant did not have but one talent because he had failed to use his opportunity to gain more. It is a fact of life that such a course brings loss. Those who are not industrious lose to those are. The spiritual application is that those who accomplish good through diligent service to God will be rewarded, while those who make no diligent effort and accomplish no good will lose everything. They will meet the fate described in verse 30.

The lesson of the parable is that God will hold us accountable for how we have used our opportunities, just as the master in the parable held his servants accountable for how they used the money he gave them. The fate of the one-talent man shows that we can be lost not just for doing evil things, but for failing to do the good that we have opportunity to do. The one-talent man violated no prohibition. Let us not only avoid the things that are condemned; let us do the things that are commanded.

Questions

1. The man who was traveling to a far country entrusted _____ talents to one servant, _____ talents to another servant, and _____ talent to a third servant.

2. How many servants used their opportunities to make gain for the master? _____

3. Who is represented by the master? _____
   The servants? _____

4. What are some of the things our Lord expects of his servants during his absence? _____

   _____

5. What event is represented by the master's return and his "reckoning" with his servants? _____

6. Why was the master as pleased with the servant who had gained only two talents as he was with the one who had gained five? _____

   _____

7. Why might the Lord be as pleased with one who visits and encourages a sick person as he is with one who pays all of that sick person's medical bills? _____

8. Why might the Lord be pleased with one whose teaching efforts are limited to handing out tracts, yet be displeased with another whose teaching efforts are similarly limited?_____

   _____

9. To account for his failure, did the one-talent man give (a) a legitimate reason or (b) an unreasonable excuse? _____

10. Do you think that in verse 26, the master was (a) admitting that he

really was the kind of master the servant had accused him of being or (b) repeating the words of the servant to show the absurdity of the servant's excuse? _____

11. By what two words did the master describe the one-talent servant?

_____

12. When Jesus speaks of the "one that hath" (v. 29) he is speaking of one who has made gain through what means? _____

_____

13. What was the fate of the unprofitable servant? _____

_____

14. What forbidden act of wickedness had the one-talent servant done?

_____

15. In the parable of the Good Samaritan were the priest and Levite guilty of (a) performing a prohibited act or (b) failing to use an opportunity to do good? _____

16. If you avoided every act that the New Testament prohibits, would you necessarily be saved? _____

17. Paul said that we are to do good to all men as we have _____ (Gal. 6:10).

18. We are to be _____ of good works (Tit. 2:14) and _____ to every good work (Tit. 3:1), for we were created in Christ unto _____ _____ (Eph. 2:10).

19. Are our good works (a) deeds that earn eternal life or (b) necessary expressions of the faith that God requires (Eph. 2:8-9; Jas. 2:17-26; Gal. 5:6)? _____

www.ingramcontent.com/pod-product-compliance
Lightning Source LLC
Chambersburg PA
CBHW021140020426
42331CB00005B/850